THE REAL SPOUSE TO BE:
The ultimate secret to enjoy good relationship for a successful marriage

Kenneth Pease

Table of contents

Chapter 1

Draw your partner to you

Each partner has to be regarded like Cinderella or Prince Charming as a relationship advances in years. However, some allies don't put out the necessary effort to maintain their attractiveness and appeal over the long term. They fail to focus on the most effective way to appeal to their partner more.

If you have no clue how to consistently be more attractive, you have stumbled onto the proper article. Here are a few persuasive ideas to help you captivate your partner and win their love all over again.

What makes a character alluring?

These qualities make others want to be around you, which makes you feel like a worthy dating partner.Your personality may have more charm if you have an attractive and generally well-kept look. So it doesn't hurt to focus on your appearance as well.

When a relationship first begins, the sincere feelings are usually taken too seriously for partners to determine if one of the parties doesn't seem very appealing.

However, the attraction and sexual tension may wane as the partnership becomes more balanced. Here, it's important to consider your actions and keep things fresh.

Techniques for attracting men as a woman
If you're thinking about how to make yourself more attractive as a woman, it's usually not as difficult as you would first think. You definitely want to know that getting attractive mostly depends on your intentional efforts rather than counting on the typical advantages you were born with.
Become informed:Many friends like it when their friends are intelligent and well-read. You don't need to be an expert on every point of view; all you actually need to do is be well-informed to have meaningful dialogues. Understanding that problem

solvers are alluring because they have persuasive reasoning skills is part of learning how to be more attractive.

Take care of your hygiene: If your hygiene is declining, it's likely that your partner won't be attracted to you any more. So, if you want to seem more attractive, take care of your hygiene, make sure you always smell good, wear clean clothes, and follow other self-care advice that will make you feel more confident and seductive. Furthermore, if your partner finds you alluring and confident, they are powerless.

Try not to swarm your spouse with attention:

When friends don't allow them room to breathe, some people become discouraged. It emits the repressive or regulating forces that it contains. Therefore, let your partner interact with their friends if they want to if they have the urge to do so. Always encourage them to enjoy themselves with their friends. When you do this, you may convince your accomplice that you believe in them.

Be attentive to their activities: Putting effort into your partner's activities is important, even if your benefits and theirs don't change. Your partner will come to comprehend how much value you place on them thanks to you. You may be certain that your relationship will strengthen as a result.

Do the unexpected occasionally:Be mindful not to let your current state of mind distract you from the importance of leaping up shocks in your relationship. Being unrestricted is one way to make yourself more seductive to your partner. Your partner will love and respect you more once they see how much effort you put into making the relationship really interesting.

When you need to compliment your spouse, there are two methods you might use. Start by supporting your partner based on what they are best at and what drives them the most. Additionally, compliment them on areas where they don't have high hopes. Make sure these compliments have been carefully reviewed before offering them so you can express your feelings appropriately.

Try not to specify too many requirements:
A partner who has high expectations might end up becoming a burden. Make sure you don't make expectations that are predictable if you want to know how to be more attractive as a woman. Your partner won't think you are too dependent on them if you put more effort into finding solutions to some of your requirements or necessities.

Make following your bliss a top priority:
Focusing more intently on the things that make you happy is another effective strategy to improve your attractiveness as a woman. When you concentrate on your happiness, you will often exude joy, making you more desirable to your partner.

Start romantic activities: Don't let your partner be too eager to start romantic dinner dates, sex, or other activities with scented candles. With time, it can become a burden for them, and they might start to wonder why you won't always stand up to the plate. Offer a few commitments that make your partner feel as if you are releasing them from some weight.

Chapter 2

Establishing a target for the marriage's success

Setting goals to enhance productivity at work, one's own health, or important life milestones like financial stability is a widespread practice. We understand the importance of pursuing objectives because we have seen what is possible when we are determined and focused. Therefore, why not also make objectives for our marriage?

Setting objectives as a pair strengthens your relationship because it forces you to work together toward a shared goal. Troy has referred to us as a team from the beginning. This idea appeals to me since it's so relatable.

Each player must cooperate with the others if the team is to succeed. Although being in a fulfilled, happy marriage is a win on this side of heaven, most couples would probably agree that your ultimate objective in marriage is to assist one another become pure and enter paradise.

How therefore can we succeed in marriage? We all have setbacks in life and sometimes lose sight of the fact that we are teammates. If you want to win, don't forget that you are on the same team. The fact that I am reminded of this encourages me to let go of whatever grudges I may be harboring and move more quickly toward reconciliation. Make a list of things you can do each day or even each week to remind one another that you are teammates. You might perhaps conduct a marriage examination of conscience, either alone in your heart or as a pair, in a manner similar to that of a daily examination of conscience. Consider what you did to show your spouse love that day or that week, as well as what you might have done better. Make a strategy for your marriage game. Every team has a strategy they work to implement that gives them the greatest chance of succeeding. What proactive steps can you take to strengthen your marriage? What barriers should you erect around your marriage to prevent harm from occurring?

Team members are held responsible for one another. The whole team is impacted if one team member makes a mistake. The need of forgiving one another while yet holding one another responsible is the same in a marriage. There is a distinction between harboring resentment and holding your spouse responsible for an injustice that requires rectification. Your team can't function cohesively until this is done. You must accept responsibility for your mistakes if you want to have a happy marriage. You shouldn't have to beg for an apology from your spouse; doing so lessens the authenticity of the apology. Recognize your errors so you won't have to continuously play defense. Forgiveness can let you leave the offending area if you are the offended spouse. For the sake of your marriage, your family, and your salvation, make it a mission to be responsible to one another.

When one player on a team is injured, another player steps forward to fill in. Learning how to better assist your spouse when they're sad is a nice goal you could decide to establish for your marriage. Are you kind and empathetic? Do you assist them in getting up or do you choose to ignore their plight so you won't have to deal with it? Perhaps you find it difficult to support your spouse while he or she is struggling because of your own scars, pride, or lack of energy. When this happens, depending on the sacrament of marriage's grace will allow you the courage to keep your marital vows "in good times and in bad."

Setting shared objectives and seeing them through will keep you intentionally connected and prevent you from drifting away.

Be flexible and set attainable objectives. Do what suits you, but keep in mind the time of year. Spend time periodically reviewing your objectives and, if required, revising your strategy. The essential thing to remember is to get back on track as quickly as you can and make allowances if a curveball is thrown your way. Life occurs, and something will undoubtedly force you to veer off course. Celebrate your successes.

Setting goals together enhances communication and helps partners comprehend one another since it gives each partner a chance to share their own hopes and aspirations for the union. Since everyone's needs are respected and heard, there are less misunderstandings, conflicts, and feelings of resentment. A happier and more satisfying marriage results from this.
interacting with one another

Spending good time together is key to finding strategies to keep a relationship alive. By keeping up their dating, happy couples establish solid bonds with one another. They create special rituals, spend time together, have fun, and seek out new experiences. They collaborate to identify interests that appeal to both of them. A successful marriage is built on a foundation of shared beliefs, interests, and aspirations, and a healthy marriage has a nice balance of freedom and togetherness.

How long should you guys be together? There are many different responses to that query, but the best researchers typically say, "As much as you can." Some mention a weekly sum. The suggested weekly schedule ranges from eight to fifteen hours.

The amount of time husbands and spouses spend together is obviously just one aspect of the problem. For the health of your relationship, quality is also essential.

Regularity, variation, adventure, and enjoyment are at least four essential components of the kind of connection that fosters a thriving marriage. Let's look more closely at each of them.

Regularity

Marriage should provide plenty of chances for couples to spend time together. On the contrary, they have to be part of the fabric of a couple's lives. That entails prioritizing family time. And doing things together demands intentionality since they don't simply "happen."

This is why it's so crucial to schedule frequent trips and date evenings, and to take whatever steps are necessary to ensure that these commitments are consistently followed (such as hiring babysitters or making time out of a hectic work schedule). The bride in Song of Solomon could serve as an inspiration for both spouses: "By night on my bed I sought the one I love; I sought him but did not find him. I said, "I will get up right now and wander the city, looking for the one I love on the streets and in the squares. Solomon's Song, verses 3 and 2. To put it another way, you must learn to seek one another like you did before becoming married. You must decide to battle for the opportunity to spend time with one another sharing your feelings, your aspirations, and your goals.

Variety

According to recent studies, happy husbands and wives benefit from each other's companionship in terms of strength, vitality, and life. Of course, this does not imply that they are always together. Breathing space is necessary for thriving, healthy partnerships. They need the ebb and flow of individuality and community. By allowing for novelty and diversity and including an element of the unexpected into your date night plans, you may integrate this sort of experience into your marriage. Add a little dash of spice every now and then to keep things interesting and keep everyone happy to be together. "Thinking outside the box" is the key. To put it another way, getting the appropriate balance is important. It's like establishing your dancing beat and then inventing moves for fun. It's crucial to change the routine to keep things new, even if it only means traveling to a different movie theater or dining at a different restaurant once a week.

Variety adds an element of adventure and excitement to a couple's time together. However, a trip might be adventurous without being large, spectacular, hazardous, or outrageous. It just has to have a hint of anything novel, odd, or surprising. This may be done in quiet, unobtrusive ways, as we've previously mentioned. It's important to maintain a little sense of unpredictability among you so that you may take advantage of the rewarding experience of responding to novel situations as a group.

Finally, date evenings are enjoyable when they are daring and intriguing, even in subtle ways. This is necessary. New activities, according to research, stimulate the brain's reward system, resulting in feelings of excitement, exhilaration, and pleasure. I Without without realizing it, husbands and couples who enjoy one other's company enhance their ties. They provide strong incentives to remain together and keep returning for more in a hundred different ways.

Couples that manage to maintain this level of humor and enjoyment as the foundation of their union are more likely to remain together. Their marriage is solid because they can incorporate pauses into their shared experiences and keep a connection going even when they are apart. They do this by creating heartfelt customs and entertaining rituals that are filled with laughter. They are intentional about creating a blended life on a solid foundation of shared values, interests, and goals rather than simply sharing a house and a bed. Additionally, they maintain a healthy relationship by giving it room to grow and by constantly recognizing the unexpected and serendipitous aspects of life.

Chapter 3

Using it in practice

Here's a suggestion that might make your next date night an authentic "out of the box" encounter. Try going out for a "progressive meal." Make a pit stop at a restaurant famed for its appetizers to start the evening. Go on to the area's best salad bar after that. Do you want some soup? Try one of the inventive dishes at an out-of-the-way café that specializes in them. From there, you may visit a restaurant renowned for its delectable entrée and go directly to the main meal. Pick your favorite ice cream store, a specialty bakery, or another eatery that offers classy desserts as your dessert destination. Better still, if you can do this on foot. Choose a picturesque route if you must drive to make the most of your travel time.

Cook Meals Together: Of course, when you get to work in the kitchen, crack up a bottle of wine or turn on some enticing music.Cooking meals together is one of the finest relationship pieces of advice for spending quality time together when you both have hectic schedules.

Try to spice things up by cooking a sophisticated French cuisine or a four-course dinner together. This is not only a good way to spend time with your friends, but it also fosters cooperation.If all goes according to plan, you'll have a romantic dinner for two at home that you made with your own two hands. Even if the meal doesn't come out as you had anticipated, you will undoubtedly laugh and make new memories with your loved ones.

Make Date Nights a Habit:
Spending quality time together increases a couple's feeling of satisfaction and reduces stress.

Include a date night in your weekly schedule as one of the most important relationship tips for a happy marriage.
A weekly date night might make your relationship appear more intriguing and help minimize relationship boredom, according to the National Marriage Project. Additionally, it enhances your sexual life, reduces the likelihood of divorce, and fosters good communication.

Let go and forget

One of the most important marital tools is the capacity to forgive and move on from previous wrongs. Being able to forgive is also a method to maintain your mental and physical health. In fact, one of the most crucial methods to keep you and your marriage intact is via forgiveness and letting go. Even when a marriage cannot survive a particular violation, forgiveness may still be useful.

Health Advantages

You are wasting your time and your energy if you continue to harbor past wounds, disappointments, trivial annoyances, betrayals, insensitivity, and wrath. If you harbor your pain (actual or imagined) for too long, it may ultimately develop into hatred and intense bitterness.

You might get exhausted from not forgiving others. Being unforgiving has a negative impact on one's body and mind. As resentment grows, the basis of your well-being and your connection is weakened. Instead, express your emotions. The act of forgiving someone has been shown to lower blood pressure, lower cholesterol, enhance sleep, lessen pain, and minimize levels of stress, anxiety, and despair. Studies have also shown that forgiving others has significant advantages.

Forgiveness is necessary for marriage, as it is for other intimate relationships. Keep in mind that errors are inevitable. Everybody has awful or cranky days. Most people sometimes say things they don't mean. One must both forgive and be forgiven.

This is particularly true if the person who injured you is trying to atone for their actions and ask for forgiveness; it is harder if your spouse is not contrite. Even so, you could still see the benefit in asking for forgiveness. Without forgiveness, no good relationship, especially a marriage can last for a very long time. But keep in mind that repentance does not entail forgiveness. Release of resentment is a process that involves making a deliberate choice to forgive. You and your spouse may benefit from forgiveness by receiving the means to process and move on. Although it may be challenging for you, forgiveness is essential in the long run. If you are married, you have experienced it. Your spouse offended you with something they said or did. It might be a little betrayal or a significant one. Your pride begs you to exact revenge in either case. If you don't respond right away, you should at least store the following "guilt card" in your pocket for when you do: "Oh yes, but what about the time when you"

The last thing we want to do after being insulted is let it go. And yet, it is precisely what we must do if we want to have a happy, long-lasting marriage. ** Here are seven ideas to keep in mind if your partner disappoints you.

DO NOT BEGIN WITHOUT YOUR PARTNER.

Don't simply corner your spouse and barge in suddenly if you need to speak to them about anything. That encourages antagonism. Instead, decide on a time to talk about the matter as a group. That will allow you both time to consider it beforehand, which will lead to a more fruitful debate than if one partner just berates the unwitting "offender."

HANDLE NEGATIVE EMOTIONS RESPONSIBLY.

We often say and do things later on that we regret when we behave passionately. Delaying the conversation until you've calmed down, gotten some perspective, and prayed about your attitude is often the wisest course of action. This will enable you to approach it with an open mind and seek a resolution rather than going in overwhelmed by your own pain. You must appreciate one another's need to "take five" as partners. Don't pursue the matter if your spouse needs a few minutes, or perhaps a day or two, to calm down. This should not be an excuse to completely avoid the conversation, but it is preferable to take some time to collect your thoughts than to let your emotions lead you in a direction that you don't want to go.

WORK ON ONE ITEM AT A TIME

Do you recall the "guilt card" we previously mentioned? You'll be tempted to whip it out after you've entered the conversation. As you compete with one another for the most offensive things the other person has ever said or done, your discussion quickly devolves into a lengthy list of transgressions. This simply exacerbates the argument and widens your differences. To be given a long list of things that need to improve might sometimes be demoralizing. It discourages rather than encourages. Instead, just focus on one issue at a time. Making significant progress in one area of your relationship is much preferable to simply practicing everything that needs to be fixed.

SPECIFY YOUR PERSPECTIVE CLEARLY.

Allow each other some quiet time to express your worries. If you are simply exchanging insults, neither of you will truly be listening to the other since you will be too preoccupied planning your next counterpunch. When the moment comes to speak, make an effort to make your partner understand your pain or displeasure. Help them understand the reasons behind the effects that their actions and words have. The guilty spouse should also be given the chance to defend their actions or remarks. It's possible that you misread their intentions, and if that's clarified, it will help to solve the issue.

HOLD THIS ISSUE LESS IMPORTANTLY THAN YOUR RELATIONSHIP.

We often lose sight of the wider picture because we are too preoccupied with our sentiments or "rights." Contrary to popular belief, conflicts over toothpaste and toilet paper do indeed cause marriages to dissolve.

Keep in mind that your connection is what matters most. Even if you may still need to work through certain problems, you still care about each other, and caring for someone else often entails accepting their point of view.

Chapter 4

loyalty in marriage is a virtue:

Most faiths sanctify marriage and consider that marital faithfulness is an agreement after the wedding vows are exchanged. However, statistics show that you cannot depend on either subjective beliefs or formalized laws to guarantee loyalty in your marriage. Therefore, loyalty requires a fresh strategy.

The premise of the new monogamy is that you and your spouse must mutually decide to be faithful to one another. It implies that the topic of monogamy is discussed openly both at the start and throughout your marriage.

Nobody chooses to start an adulterous relationship out of the blue. Infidelity starts in the head and emotions. A person has been engaging in increasingly severe mental and emotional affairs for quite some time before actually committing physical adultery.

Similarly, marital faithfulness starts well before the wedding day. Before marriage ever enters the picture, we first make a commitment to be a person of loyal character to ourselves. When we get engaged, we make a commitment to our future spouse, and when we get married, we renew that vow. Marriage faithfulness is the everyday decision to put your spouse and family first.

Increasing Marital Integrity

Marriage faithfulness is improved when you support your spouse, pay attention to what they have to say, and try to fulfill their needs. Setting sensible limits for your media use and your interactions with people outside the home also helps to enhance it.

Now, if you ask around, you'll discover that the majority of people automatically associate the term "fidelity" with marital faithfulness. I now swear never to engage in sexual activity with anybody else. A few years into a marriage, asking your spouse for your idea of what defines having sex is is nearly always a poor indicator.

In illness and sorrow, in the sun and life's rain, for better or worse. Every married couple accepts these commitments in one way or another. Promise to be together forever, to hold each other's hands for all of time.Marriage is a unique link that brings two individuals together in a solid, enduring relationship. What happens, however, when marriages do not last forever? Why do people stop believing in themselves and look for fulfillment outside of marriage?

An unbreakable marriage is built on the foundations of trust and loyalty. If you and your partner are reliable, then your marriage will flourish like nothing else. All other aspects of marital companionship love, tenderness, care, protection, respect, and understanding automatically fit into the ideal image once trust and faithfulness are present. As a result, integrity and trust have magical consequences that make your marriage happy and radiant.

However, we often see the dissolution of marital relationships in our community as a result of adultery and betrayal. In addition to the married couples, this has an adverse effect on their family, significant others, and everyone else who is directly or indirectly tied to them. What, therefore, prevents or influences marital fidelity?

Causes of Marital Infidelity:
a lack of mutual regard, understanding, and trust
External Relationships
inability to deal with shared variations in viewpoints, ideas, mentalities, and personalities

a lack of quality time spent together a failure to fulfill one's own marriage tasks and obligations
Breaking the expectations that partners have of one another. Overly possessive and protective partners don't let their partners live their lives freely.
Disputes and miscommunication
effects of daily hazels, tensions, and stress
Third-party involvement
As I said earlier, adultery and breach of trust in a marriage cause unimaginable suffering and disruption in the life of the married couple and his family members. Additionally, this causes a variety of physical and psychological disorders, including:
Physical unease and agitation
alterations to nutrition and sleeping habits
a lack of cleanliness and personal care.

How to Promote Marriage Fidelity;
Mutual understanding: You may better cultivate loyalty in your marriage by getting

to know your partner. Most marriages end in divorce because of a lack of communication between the partners. Don't allow it to occur in your life as well. The fundamental and most important element of having a marriage blossom with trust and commitment is mutual understanding.

Mutual Sharing: If you wish to discuss your feelings, hopes, ideas, and points of view with your spouse. Then do it, please! Be honest about your feelings and don't assume your spouse will share them. Your hearts and thoughts are connected by your mutual sharing. Additionally, it is the surest way to inspire loyalty in your marriage union.

Mutual respect: Let's face it, nobody is perfect. In actuality, we all aspire to and live in perfection. The same weaknesses and strengths that you have as an individual also apply to your spouse. As a result, respecting one another's differences is yet another way to improve your marriage's fidelity rate.

Be a spouse after being a friend: If you tend to dominate or be bossy with your spouse, this could harm your marriage and drive your partner away from you. Be your partner's closest friend first, and everything else will fall into place on its own. We all need to be among people that make us feel safe, protected, and welcomed rather than condemned and degraded!

Spend "quality" time with your partner: No matter how much time you have together, make the most of it. In this fast-paced world we seldom find time for our spouse. We sometimes take them for granted as well. People, this is not fair! Your spouse also needs your undivided attention. Spend your time together, even if it is just for ten minutes, with love, care, trust, passion, and understanding.

Rejoice and revitalize: For some couples, marriage can become routine after a certain amount of time has passed. The main cause of infidelity in marriages is this. Instead of looking for that chemistry and pleasure elsewhere, strive to infuse your marriage with the same charm. Spend time with one another, go on a vacation together, and give unexpected presents. In other words, celebrate and re-energize your own marriage so that there won't be room for anyone else to enter.

Do not cheat: It is best to talk to a trusted friend or family member about your feelings for someone outside of your marriage and to seek professional help from a counselor or psychologist if you feel that your marriage is having trouble.
Exchange presents as a sign of appreciation.

Gift-giving and receiving:These are likely the love languages that are misunderstood the most. Some people can see it as being ungrateful or as the receiver being preoccupied on goods rather than love. That's not the case, however.

If you or your partner express your love via presents, it suggests that you experience love in the form of a material good.

It doesn't matter whether that thing is a 50-foot ship or a little trinket from a charity shop. Either way, the message is the same: I saw this and thought of you. I think about you all the time. In this view, feeling rather than excess is the fundamental essence of giving gifts. The present may be more meaningful to someone who uses this love language than to someone who uses a different love language. It provides a constant reminder that they are loved every time they see it.

We often use the same love language with our spouses as we do with ourselves. , it's probable that your partner's love language is gift-giving if they purchase an album for you two days after you express your passion for a new band or if they purchase a membership to a magazine they believe you'll like. Observing how your spouse responds to gifts is another effective approach to determine whether that person speaks to you in terms of gifts. According to Williams, if someone feels humiliated upon receiving a gift, it's probably not their love language. On the other hand, if they show extreme enthusiasm, showcase the item, wear it every day, or brag about it to their friends, they probably feel really appreciated by the gesture.

Examples of how a person who speaks this love language might show their affection include:
sending flowers to their lover, even if there is no specific occasion.
purchasing their partner's preferred snack item during grocery shopping.
obtaining tickets for their companion to watch their preferred performer or artist.

presenting their significant other with a gift card to a restaurant they had been meaning to explore.
requesting delivery of their partner's lunch or coffee while they are at work.
leaving a little token of appreciation for their partner to discover when they awaken.

If your partner uses the gift's love language, even if you don't naturally speak it, it's still important to try learning it.

"Look at everything in your everyday life through the lens of gift-giving, much as you apply a filter to an Instagram photo."

If you drive by a bakery on your way home from work every day, consider the thought that "My spouse truly feels appreciated when I bring them presents" and stop there for a treat before returning home."

Chapter 5

Effective communication promote good relationship

Relationship communication is like a river. It's enjoyable, feels good, and supports everyone around when ideas and sentiments between spouses flow easily. However, communication flow that is tumultuous has the potential to be harmful. And as a result of communication breakdowns, tension increases. Then, when the words begin to flow once more, they frequently do so abruptly and in a destructive deluge.

Couples sometimes avoid unpleasant talks because they find it difficult to communicate well as a married pair, especially when it comes to significant concerns. Without ever engaging in the talks that are genuinely most essential to them, they exchange snippets of information about who is going where when and who will pick up the kids.

What constitutes effective communication in a marriage? In a strong relationship, partners communicate honestly, freely, and with confidence, expressing even their most intimate ideas. When obstacles happen, they speak their worries and emotions with ease and consideration, and when things are going well, they speak their optimistic views. Both parties speak politely, steering clear of derogatory, upsetting, or domineering remarks. Instead of finding fault with what their spouse has to say or discounting what they hear, even if they have a different viewpoint, they pay close attention and strive to comprehend what they are hearing with sympathy. After speaking, the couple feels satisfied with the dialogue and that their issues have been taken into account and handled.

People who strive for perfection are wary of making mistakes. High standards are known to exist among them. This can prevent you from communicating important information to your companions. This is due to the possibility that you wouldn't feel comfortable disclosing even the most basic facts to them.

More important than the "blockbuster" material is the minute information given and discussed in a relationship.

By including them in your hobbies, sharing this knowledge with your spouse fosters a strong romantic relationship.

www.ingramcontent.com/pod-product-compliance
Lightning Source LLC
LaVergne TN
LVHW020528160826
845677LV00015B/3964

* 9 7 9 8 3 5 3 0 7 7 2 2 0 *